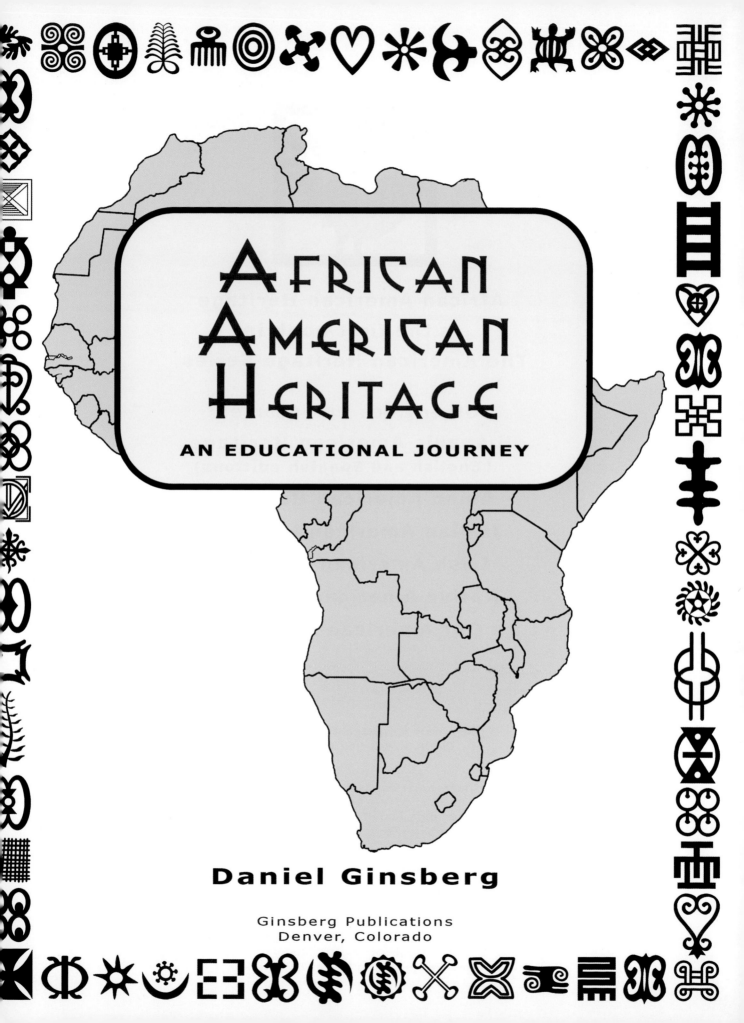

African American Heritage

AN EDUCATIONAL JOURNEY

Daniel Ginsberg

Ginsberg Publications
Denver, Colorado

**African American Heritage
is the first book in
The American Heritage Series.**

Other titles will include:

**Hispanic American Heritage
(English and Spanish editions)**

Asian American Heritage

Italian American Heritage

Irish American Heritage

Native American Heritage

Our American Heritage

African American Heritage
ISBN: 978-0-9623284-4-2

Also available are
The African American Heritage Coloring Book
ISBN: 978-0-9623284-3-5
The Teacher's Activity Handbook and CD
ISBN: 978-0-9623284-5-9

Published in 2016 by Ginsberg Publications
2616 Fairfax Street, Denver, Colorado 80207
Text, Illustrations & Photography by Daniel Ginsberg
Copyright © 2016 by Daniel Ginsberg
All rights reserved

www.GinsbergPublications.com
A Veteran Owned Company
Printed in the United States of America

TABLE OF CONTENTS

NYAME NTI
This Adinkra depicts a stalk of grain which symbolizes that food is the basis of life and that people could not survive if God had not placed food here on Earth for nourishment.

Today we know that all of mankind began it's journey into the future in the Afar Region of Ethiopia.

It is from here that our ancestors traveled and explored and spread to every corner of the earth.

Likewise, it is from this same Afar Region, that all the people, of all the villages, of all the tribal groups that we call African originated.

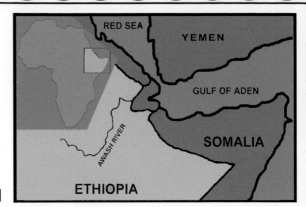

Come, explore in both text and illustrations, the history and the heritage of our American ancestors of African descent.

The African-American Journey is an epic story. Similar to other cultures that have endured the inhumanity of slavery, today, you can be proud of their heritage of hard-working people and the significant contributions made by so many that have come before.

Their inventiveness, creativity, dedication and unending willingness to improve mankind continues to be an inspiration that is appreciated by all the nations of the world.

"Heritage" refers to the legacy of attributes and customs inherited from past generations. Both intangible attributes, such as folklore and traditions, coupled with historical records, like art and artifacts combine to tell the story of the cultural heritage of a society.

This Adinkra, is an African symbol of the Sankofa Bird that is often seen in Akan art. It represents the need for people to reflect on their past and on their heritage so that they can successfully build a meaningful future.

Tribal People of Africa

The tribal people of Africa are as varied as the continent they've lived on since man's beginning.

Though the cultures on the continent have evolved and many tribes have modernized, they still maintain a strong connection with their cultural heritage which remains a powerful source of pride.

Masai

Today, there are more than 400 tribes that vary from stone-age cultures to modern 21st Century individuals.

From the tall, elegant Masai, who raise their cattle in traditional villages on the East African savannah to the tiny, forest-dwelling Pygmy people, the tribes of Africa now live peacefully with their neighbors while maintaining their own language, customs, and history.

Surma

Peul

Pokot

Mursi

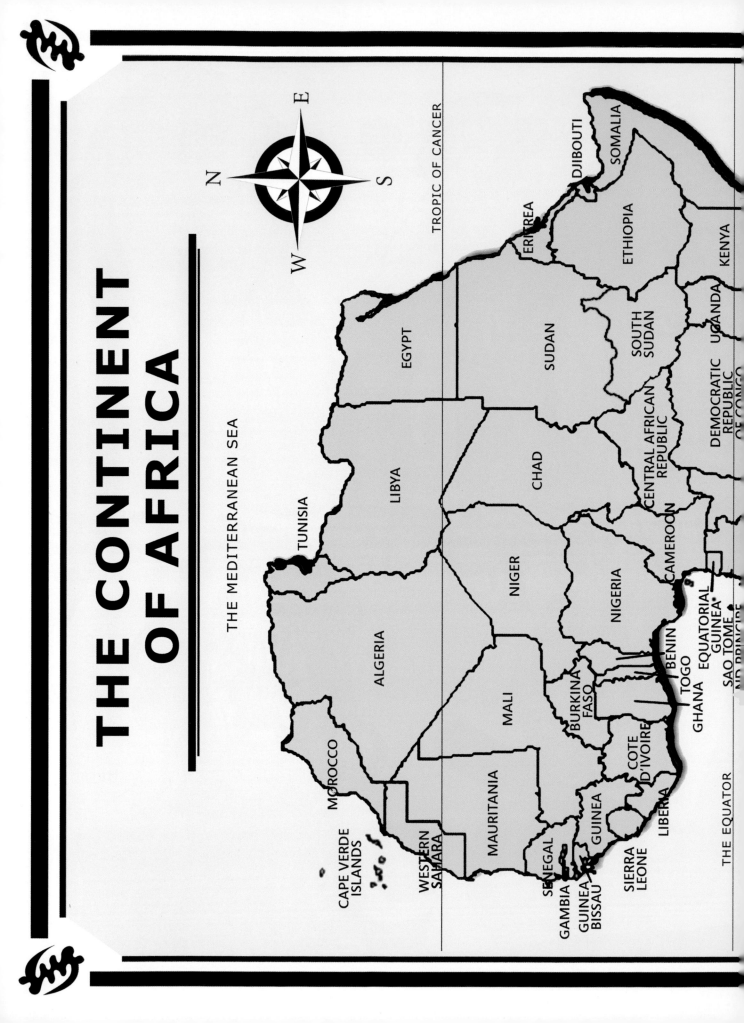

THE CONTINENT OF AFRICA

THE MEDITERRANEAN SEA

TROPIC OF CANCER

THE EQUATOR

N E S W

TUNISIA

MOROCCO

ALGERIA

LIBYA

EGYPT

WESTERN SAHARA

MAURITANIA

MALI

NIGER

CHAD

SUDAN

SOUTH SUDAN

ERITREA

DJIBOUTI

SOMALIA

ETHIOPIA

KENYA

UGANDA

CENTRAL AFRICAN REPUBLIC

DEMOCRATIC REPUBLIC OF CONGO

CAMEROON

NIGERIA

BURKINA FASO

BENIN

TOGO

GHANA

EQUATORIAL GUINEA*

SAO TOME AND PRINCIPE

COTE D'IVOIRE

LIBERIA

SIERRA LEONE

GUINEA

GUINEA BISSAU

GAMBIA

SENEGAL

CAPE VERDE ISLANDS

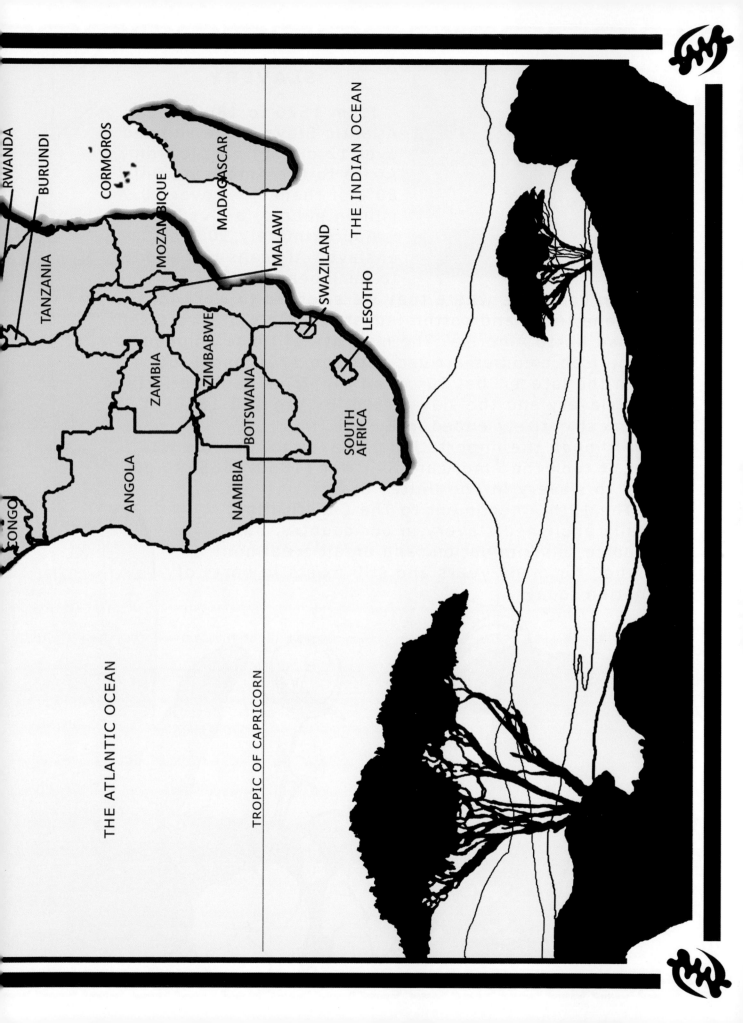

RWANDA

BURUNDI

CORMOROS

MADAGASCAR

MOZAMBIQUE

TANZANIA

MALAWI

SWAZILAND

LESOTHO

THE INDIAN OCEAN

ZIMBABWE

ZAMBIA

BOTSWANA

SOUTH
AFRICA

ANGOLA

NAMIBIA

CONGO

THE ATLANTIC OCEAN

TROPIC OF CAPRICORN

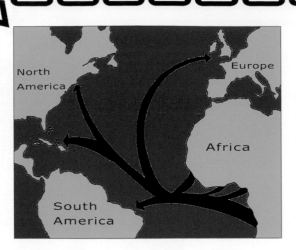

SLAVERY

From 1526 to 1867, the Atlantic Slave Trade shipped over 12 million people from Africa to the Americas. Only 80% of them, just over 10.7 million people, arrived alive.

Approximately 90% of enslaved Africans were sent to Caribbean and South American countries where they were forced to work in sugar cane, rice, and cotton industries. Only 6% were sent to British North America. The majority of those shipped to the American colonies arrived between 1720 and 1780.

In the late 1700s, European countries began efforts to end slavery and the slave trade. By the mid-1800s it was almost entirely ended in Europe.

Although the importation of slaves to America was ended, it took the American Civil War (1860-1865) to put an end to slavery in The United States.

The 13th Amendment to The Constitution, officially abolished slavery in our country, but predjudice, discrimination, and unfair treatment continued for many years and still exists in parts of our nation today.

Many slaves, men, women, and children, lived lives of extreme hardship without any civil rights or the possibility of improving their situation.

Today, there are places in the world where this inhumane system still exists.

Desegregation of all American institutions was an important issue during the Civil Rights Movement. Of special importance was the desegregation of the American public school system, universities, and the military.

President Abraham Lincoln issued the Emancipation Proclamation on January 1, 1863. The proclamation declared "that all persons held as slaves" within the rebellious states "are, and henceforth shall be free."

Emancipation & Desegregation

Rosa Parks refused to give up her seat on the bus and has been known as "The First Lady of American Civil Rights" ever since.

Harriet Tubman escaped from slavery to become a leading abolitionist before and during the Civil War.

Frederick Douglass escaped from slavery to become an orator, a writer, a statesman, and a leader of the abolitionist movement.

The Edmund Pettus Bridge was the site of a bloody conflict when armed policemen attacked civil rights demonstrators as they were marching to the Alabama state capital of Montgomery.

US BRIDGE

Reverend Martin Luther King, Jr. was a Baptist minister, activist, and leader in the American Civil Rights Movement. He is best known for his role in the advancement of civil rights using non-violent civil disobedience based on his Christian beliefs.

In Uniform

Since the time of The American Revolution, men and women of color have served in the military with honor and with great courage.

Today African Americans continue to be a major presence in all five branches of The United States Armed Forces.

Hazel Johnson-Brown was a nurse and educator who served with the Army from 1955-1983.
In 1979 she became the first black female general in the United States Army and the first black chief of the United States Army Nurse Corps.

The Medal of Honor was created during the American Civil War and is the highest military decoration presented by the United States government to a member of its armed forces. A recipient must have distinguished themself, at the risk of their own life, above and beyond the call of duty.
Eighty-nine African Americans have been awarded the Medal of Honor.
Robert Augustus Sweeney is only one of thirteen Americans to have been awarded the Medal of Honor twice.

On Stage and Screen

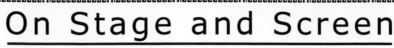

It is impossible to present all the fantastic entertainers that have contributed to so rich a heritage. Here are only a few that changed our world of entertainment.

PORGY AND BESS

Sammy Davis Jr. was a supremely talented entertainer:

a dancer, singer, actor of stage and screen, impressionist, comedian, and musician.

Porgy and Bess is an American English language opera. It was first performed in New York City on Sept. 30, 1935, and featured an entire cast of classically trained African-American singers. Today's performances are still 100% African American.

John "Dizzy" Gillespie was an improvisational jazz trumpeter, bandleader, and composer and is considered one of the greatest jazz trumpeters of all time. **13**

Hattie McDaniel was an actress, songwriter, singer, and comedian. She became the first African American to win an Oscar (1940) for her role as Mammy in "Gone with the Wind."

Both Michael Jackson and Prince were multi-talented singers and songwriters. They were musical innovators with flamboyant stage presence.

Marian Anderson, 1897-1993, was one of the most celebrated singers of the 20th century and an important figure in the struggle for black artists to overcome racial prejudice.

She sang at the Lincoln Memorial on April 9, 1939.

14

Scientists and Inventors

For more than 300 years, black inventors have served as pioneers in the field of science and industry, making enormous impacts on our society and the world.

As African Americans sought freedom and equality, many among them, scientists, educators and even slaves, developed the tools and processes that helped to shape the modern agricultural, industrial, and technological landscape.

It would be impossible to show, or even list, all of their contributions and inventions. Here are only a few that you might recognize.

For more information, go to www.famousscientists.org

In the 1750s, using only a pocket knife, 22 year old Benjamin Banneker created the first clock made in America.
His wooden clock kept accurate time for 20 years.

George Washington Carver, 1864–1943,
discovered more than 300 uses for
peanuts, sweet potatoes, pecans, and soybeans:
shoe polish, lubricants, shaving cream,
and women's face makeup were
only a few of his many discoveries.
He is considered one of
America's greatest scientists.

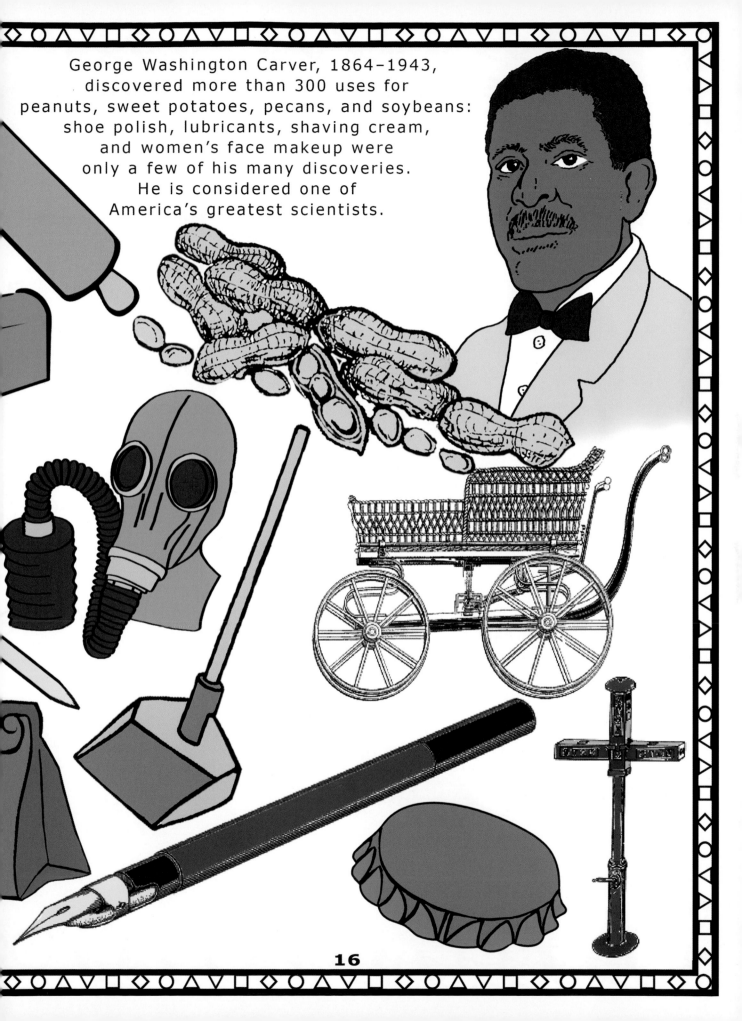

Sports

No group, anywhere in the world, has made more of an impact on sports than have African-American athletes.

Today, they continue to set the bar high for excellence in every area of sports, are involved at every level of competition, and hold more sports records than any other ethnicity.

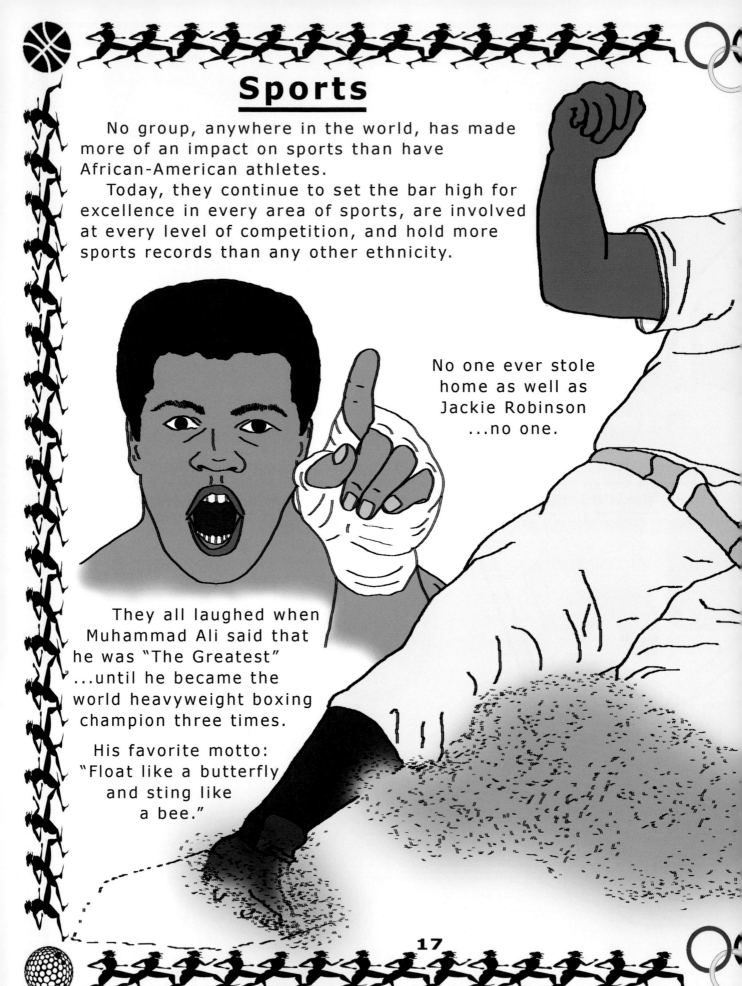

No one ever stole home as well as Jackie Robinson ...no one.

They all laughed when Muhammad Ali said that he was "The Greatest" ...until he became the world heavyweight boxing champion three times.

His favorite motto: "Float like a butterfly and sting like a bee."

Florence Griffith-Joyner... known as Flo-Jo, was a track and field athlete and is considered the fastest woman of all time.

In 1988, she set the world records for both the 100m and 200m dashes. Both records still stand today.

Flo-Jo was also known for the line of sport fashions she designed.

Her motto was: "Look good, feel good, run fast."

Jackie Robinson broke through major league baseball's color barrier with courage, hard work and his God-given talents.

"We all have dreams. To make dreams come into reality, it takes an awful lot of dedication determination, effort, and self-discipline."
Jesse Owens

At the 1936 Olympic Games in Berlin, Germany, Jesse Owens won four track and field gold medals.
He was the most successful athlete at the games and is credited with "single-handedly crushing Hitler's myth of Aryan supremacy.

Literature and the Arts

African-American literature and art are known worldwide for their diversity of style and depth of content.

ROOTS
The Saga of an American Family
ALEX HALEY

Look at art.
Create art.
It's all around you.
It's everywhere.

ZORA NEALE HURSTON

THEIR EYES WERE
WATCHING GOD

A NOVEL

Maya Angelou
I Know
Why the
Caged Bird
Sings

Read a book...
Then read another.
Write...
Tell a story.

Today and Tomorrow

Today, African Americans live and thrive in every town and city, work in every industry and in every profession in America.

Condoleezza Rice is a political scientist and diplomat, who served as the 66th United States Secretary of State. She was the first female African-American Secretary of State.

James Smith, better known as LL Cool J, began rapping on the streets of Queens, New York.

Today, he is a respected recording artist, actor, and TV personality.

Who are your role models?

Misty Copeland became the first African-American woman to be promoted to principal dancer in the American Ballet Theater's 75 year history.

James Earl Jones stuttered as a child. Today, he is known as "one of American's greatest actors." You may know him as the voice of Mufasa in The Lion King or as Darth Vader in Star Wars.

Oprah Winfrey was born into poverty but through hard work, she rose to become a media proprietor, talk show host, actress, producer, and philanthropist. She was awarded the Presidential Medal of Freedom and honorary doctorate degrees from Duke and Harvard Universities.

"For centuries, African American
men and women have persevered to enrich
our national life and bend the arc of history
toward justice.
From resolute Revolutionary War soldiers
fighting for liberty to the hardworking students
of today reaching for horizons their ancestors
could only have imagined,
African Americans have strengthened our nation
by leading reforms, overcoming obstacles and
breaking down barriers."

PRESIDENT BARACK OBAMA